MY LIFE PAINTED WITH WORDS

BY LILETTA HARLEM

Copyright © 2021 by Liletta Harlem All rights reserved. No part of this publication may be reproduced, stored in a retrieval system, or transmitted in any form or by any means, electronic, mechanical, scanning, recording, photocopying, or otherwise, without the prior written permission of the author.

Limit of Liability/Disclaimer of Warranty: This publication is designed to provide accurate and authoritative information regarding the subject matter covered. It is sold with the understanding that neither the author nor the publisher is engaged in rendering legal, investment, accounting, or other professional services. While the publisher and author have used their best efforts in preparing this book, they make no representations or warranties with respect to the accuracy or completeness of the contents of this book and specifically disclaim any implied warranties of merchantability or fitness for a particular purpose. No warranty may be created or extended by sales representatives or written sales materials.

The advice and strategies contained herein may not be suitable for your situation. You should consult with a professional when appropriate. Neither the publisher nor the author shall be liable for any loss of profit or any other commercial damages, including but not limited to special, incidental, consequential, personal, or other damages.

My Life Painted With Words by Liletta Harlem

Paperback ISBN: 978-1-7348617-5-4

Illustrator Kelly Haneklau

Printed in the United States of America www.lilettaharlem.com

TABLE OF CONTENTS

INTRODUCTION 1

WINTER 3

    LOST MINDS 4

    EMPTINESS 6

    DEAR DAD, ... 8

    TWO LINES 10

    DADDY'S LITTLE 12

    MY UNBORN 14

    DON'T SAY YOU LOVE ME 15

    CHASING THE 17

    THE MOURNING AFTER 19

    TORN 21

SPRING 22

    I'M ONLY HUMAN 23

    CHANGE 25

    SOMETIMES 26

    BROWN SKIN 27

    #GOALS 30

    JUST ME 31

SUMMER 34

    HUMBLE BEGINNINGS 35

    VALIDATION 36

    I WANT TO 37

    YOU 40

    FOREVER LOVE 41

AUTUMN 42
   CLOSURE 43
   BROKEN VASE - THE CYCLE OF LIFE 44
   MY LOVE - THE PERFECT LOVE STORY! 48
   FRIENDSHIP 51
   YOUR SEASON IS NOW! 53

INTRODUCTION

I never considered myself a poet!
I just knew that I loved the way that words danced
across the page and told my story.
Rhythmic sounds expressing pain, giving
permission to feel and heal.
The page is my palette the words are my paintbrush.
Welcome to my life painted with words!

I've been writing for years, but I find I do the most writing when I'm going through a painful moment. There's something therapeutic about pouring your emotions out in written form that draws me in and moves me to write.

When I decided to create a book of my writings, I knew it had to be more than just simply a book of poems. That's when it hit me, why not make this book a complement to my new book, **The *Power Resides at the end of I Am*** ? The *"Power"* book as I call it, is all about embracing the seasons of our life.

My Life Painted With Words are raw unedited selections of my poetry from the various personal seasons of my life. My

Liletta Harlem

personal quotes for each season are what the various times of my life have meant in those seasons.

Complementing my poetry are a few beautiful images created by the amazing artist, Kelly Haneklau. I'm forever thankful for her contribution to this project!

Thank you for joining my journey and I pray that you feel heard and seen as you read along.

WINTER

"The Winter can be cold and brutal but there is growth happening at the core!"

Liletta Harlem

LOST MINDS

A STORY OF MEMORY LOSS
I walk along a path
Taking the scenic route for a sense of the familiar
But the journey feels peculiar
Images mean everything and yet nothing
Empty outlines of memories that no longer exist
I stop to smell the flowers that I can't resist
And I seem to remember the scent should mean something
And in an instant the connection is missed
If I can't remember the why's
Then am I still even me
Do I hold my mind accountable?
Or do I set it free
When my loved ones look at me with care
Will I eventually answer with an empty stare?
When I look up at the heavens will I know who's there
My prayer-
That my loved ones never stop loving me
And that my God remembers me
Even when I have no more memories

Liletta Harlem

EMPTINESS

THE LOSS OF A BABY
I never lost something that was so much a part of me
And while emptiness can fill a room,
there's an ache when it fills a womb.
How can a loss bring so much shame?
From a child, I never got to name pained by a body that will never feel the same.
Will I forever think of what it would be at this stage?
Or who would be its friends at this age?

It's like, I want to be enraged, but
the hurt just sits in my soul encaged.

I'll never get to hear the first cry
or one last goodbye.
I'll never be awakened in the middle of the night,
or laugh about how it fell in love at first sight.

From the moment of conception, it was a part of me.
And now it's gone.
So, it's just me.
In an empty room,

with an empty womb.

Every ache and pain are normal

I assume.

even when it's my heart it consumes.

DEAR DAD,

GRIEF AND LOSS

Today's the 1-year anniversary of your death.
And,
Here's the part that's sad.
Lately, I'm grieving the things I've never had.
Like, even though our relationship wasn't bad,
I long for what we should have had
I mourn the days we didn't talk
The pictures I didn't take
The trips to the hospital I didn't make
The calls that I was so busy I missed

See if I had just one more day, I'd have us take a bunch of selfies, I'd have you tell me more about the family I never knew, just so I could hear you laugh as you try to remember and probably just make up the rest.
Dad you were the best.
And you have another grandchild!
At least that's the conversation I'm sad I never got.
The baby I never got to hold will never be the grandchild you got to see.

I'm torn because the imagined memories
hurt like they're reality
And this letter to you was supposed to be about the new baby
But instead, it's simply about me
Longing for the people that I can't see
For the memories that can never be
Just me
A year later
Holding onto a letter and a few pictures
And the memories.

Liletta Harlem

TWO LINES

THE DAY I LOST YOU
Two lines
Two lives
Yours and mine
The happiest day of my life
now cuts like a knife
I felt you
I knew you were sharing my life
My blood
My heart
And now we're apart
And I never met you
But it's like I already knew
your personality
I already saw you laughing
And smiling
You're sensitive just like me
But you analyze intellectually
Like your dad
And when your mad
You're kind of like both of us
The way you fuss

And I already knew you would love the Creator
Nothing would be greater
than telling people about our God
You get that from your mom
But the way you stay calm
That's all your dad
And see that's why I'm so sad
Because with just two lines
I saw the line
Of time
We cried at your first walk
Cheered at your first talk
We loved you through it all
Just a line
With a faint heart
But you shared my heart
Right from the start
And this pain of your loss
Feels like a lifetime of grief
I may never recover
From the cries I never heard
The kicks I never felt
I hate this hand I was dealt
Goodbye my little rice baby
8 weeks
2 lines
Goodbye…for now

DADDY'S LITTLE

ABANDONMENT ISSUES
Daddy's Little- What?
I'd like to say Girl
But that's not my world
I wasn't the one chosen to be
The princess, oh so precious daughter of mine
I was the secret
Left behind
I was the
No one knows your mine
And I'll pick the other family every time
And I grew up believing
That being the secret or other woman
Was just Fine
Because no one can have enough love for me and someone
else
So, I'll sit on the shelf
Until you need me
My mind
My body
My words

Just so long as you need me
And in that moment
It's like I'm number one
I'm the most important person
But the fun always ends
And I don't know if it's me
Or them
Because I don't truly believe I can be
Number one
So, I'm a self-fulfilling prophet
Knowing the other show will always
Drop
I look for you in every man I meet
It's pure self-defeat
If I wasn't number one to you
How could I be to them
If I was only "oh by the way" for you
Why would I ever expect to be a gem
Daddy's little
adult trying to find some way
To make it alright
To make the wrong somehow right.
Daddy's little best kept secret

MY UNBORN

GRIEVING MY CHILD
If I'd lost my sight I'd have learned to see with my ears.
If I'd lost my hearing, I'd hear with my eyes.
But there's no replacing your loss.
It's like my entire body grieves
And looks to my mind to tell it how to heal.
No other parts of me can step in and compensate for the empty womb or the broken heart.
The imagination of what you could have been is more like the memory of what you were.
My mind is trapped between the reality and the dream.
Holding on to the brief moments with you in my heart because otherwise I feel like I've betrayed you.
In just a few short weeks you were my validation and yet the biggest thief to my self-value.
If only the visions of loving you were as clear as the visions of losing you.
I am praying for peace, but I no longer know what that peace is even supposed to look like.
I feel like I'm losing it!

DON'T SAY YOU LOVE ME

DADDY ISSUES
Because those words carry the weight of every
man that never did.
They reopen wounds that never healed
Giving me a false sense of security, I don't need to feel
Don't join the long list of men that
Promised to never leave
Only to leave every time
Or bring me down so low
Leaving me to die
Please don't say you care
Because if you care you will know
That my emotional scars tattooed across my
soul cannot be removed
Although I cover them with false confidence
Big cheeky smiles of pretense
They're there
Peeking through
So please leave me be
This is the best version you will see

Liletta Harlem

The oak tree
Standing alone and powerful
Unloved
So please don't say you love me

CHASING THE

ADDICTIONS
Chasing the high
Chasing the low
Not wanting to crash
But, how low can I go.
Reckless endanger
Buried down anger
Which poison will kill me?
I never know
I sell my body
But I never gain
There's not enough substance
To cover the pain

I live for tomorrow
Because I can't face today
The voices convince me
I'm in my own way
I dance for the people
The laughs are for free
A standing ovation
For the actor playing me

Liletta Harlem

How low can I go?
Not wanting to crash
Chasing the low
Chasing the high
I pray that I wake
Before I should die
Chasing the low
Chasing the high

THE MOURNING AFTER

RELAPS: THE STRUGGLE OF AN ADDICT FIGHTING
One, Two, Three, Four
I promised I wouldn't do this anymore
One, Two,
If they only knew
3, 4
I've tried this before
I'll just give in a little this time
1, 2, 3
I take a hit again and again
I want this to stop
I know it's a sin
1, 2
I can't stop now till I reach that high
4
This was the next time
I'd promised that I would try
2, 3
I didn't mean to lie
But
The world is too much
I just need my crutch

Liletta Harlem

I promise I'll never do this again

I know I'm hurting all that I love

Especially the one above

On all that I LOVE

This is the last time

Not like last time

Like THIS time

Can't be like last time

Because that means this time

Is only the last time to another this time

And

The pain feels worse each time

I grow numb inside

I hate this person

And that's why this

Must be

The last time

TORN

LIFE WITH AN ABUSER
I'm torn between the person I imagined
 and the person you really are.
The person that knows I hate storms, and yet created mental storms through disrespect.
The person that shared my fantasies but didn't share my reality. The person that loved the way I
walked but didn't walk with me in my faith.
The one that could make me laugh so hard I would cry and yet cry so hard I'd want to die.
I love you for the good and thank you for the bad because now I know how to walk away when
I'm torn.

SPRING

"Spring brings you out of the cold and introduces you to new life!"

I'M ONLY HUMAN

FINDING MY STRENGTH
That's my superpower
But admittedly I cower
at the thought of being super.
And I'm not a hero,
because I have zero
experience in saving the day!
But in a way
I guess
When I stand up for the voiceless
and I expose my soul for the hopeless,
then I become a powerful human
And that's my superpower
But I'm only human

CHANGE

EMBRACING CHANGE

Does the caterpillar know it's changing when it's in the cocoon?

Does the butterfly ever emerge too soon?

When a snake sheds its skin, does it know how close it comes to its end?

Does a baby bird avoid the flight, simply because it's never soared
from that height?

I wonder, are we the only ones that fight change?
Are we the only ones that can't stand growing pains?

Liletta Harlem

SOMETIMES

MANAGING DEPRESSION
The strong need grace
Because sometimes the pain doesn't show on our face
But in our silence!
Sometimes the sadness in our heart needs a place to go
Sometimes we know
How to fix the broken but our minds are fragmented
with words unspoken,

We are perfectly imperfect, and we shatter the perfect picture
with acts
and inaccurate facts can fill our heads too.
In fact, we are just like you.
The strong need grace
Because sometimes it's ourselves we want to erase
And sometimes the sadness in our hearts just needs a space.

BROWN SKIN

BEING A BLACK WOMAN
Melanin
Beauty
Thick in all the right places
Our age doesn't show in our faces
They say "black don't crack"
So, at 65 we look 45
And honey
For us 40 is the new 20
At least that's what the outer image says.

But inside tells another story
To live up to expectations of strength
We hide our tears
We dare not speak of our fears

As our bodies slowly creep internally toward a biological clock
We wonder will we have that baby
Find that mate
Finally remove these burdens off our plate
Or Is it too late

Liletta Harlem

We are constantly seeking to stand out
While not appearing to stand by
Always ready to stand up
We pretend like our cup
Never runneth over

We gotta stay
Woke
Heard
Respected
Calm
Hyped
Ready to fight
For man, woman, and child

It's wild!

We tell our baby girls they are beautiful
But when they see mommy hating herself
That's the truth they keep

Ain't that deep?

Our actions don't match our words
So, commendation goes unheard
We duplicate
The same self-hate
Covered up with fake
Smiles

Black don't crack

But the weight on our backs

Is breaking us

#GOALS

THE INNER STRUGGLE

Her smile lights up the world

But she still goes dark

And her journey is no Walk in the Park

She feels the weight of other mistakes

That still make her heart ache.

She's #goals

To a few

But if only they knew

She can't see what they do

Buried under grief

The only relief

Comes in the sigh

Not in the high

JUST ME

A VOICE FOR MANY

Here I am ... just plain ole me

But sometimes it seems like there's nothing about me that's plain,

And sometimes it seems like all I feel is pain.

And yet, it's the pain of abuse, pain from being used, that makes me powerful to a few.

And it's the cuts that still bleed- that prompt me to help those in need.

And it's the hurt deep in my chest- that push me to give to others my best.

And sometimes I wish I could stop, take a minute, and on the remote to life

Push pause,

Not fight for a cause.

But life won't stand still, and time never will-

Be on my side,

so, I keep it moving; keep a smile on my face,

Trying not to lose pace.

And all the while- only against myself I race.

Because the battle is within-

Liletta Harlem

and the struggle lies with me,
And yet, I'm just plain ole me,
If I could open my mouth and sing – I would
And if I could spit out a rap – I would
Or if I could write it out in poetry form and have people snapping at my rhythm- I would.
But I'm just plain old me,
And many call me sweet, and say "you're a nice girl, and you're so blessed"
and all the time I'm giving God the glory, but deep in my heart rests another story, because being nice and being sweet don't pay bills,
and being nice and being sweet- is what got me beat-
and being nice and being sweet- is what got me knocked off my feet-
so, while I'm smiling and grinning
in my head I'm sinning,
and in my heart wishing-
that maybe
if I was just a little less sweet and a little less nice,
maybe I'd cry a little less at night,
or if I was a little less sweet and little less kind-
then maybe manipulators would play a little less with my mind
But here I am exposing myself for the world to see,
helping the women who are just like me,

trying to create a door- so that other women can flee, thanking God every day- that he allowed me to become free, - a woman, a fighter, a victim a survivor here I am- just plain ole me……

SUMMER

"Longer days and warm nights,
summer is a time for love!"

HUMBLE BEGINNINGS

HER START

His dark skin lit up with his smile

Smooth and ready to party-

He meets her

she's innocent but looking for love

He loved life and making her laugh

and she loved him for those same reasons.

Their love like a 70s love song birthed something special!

A relationship that would never die she kept a part of him in her heart and her womb

Together they created a forever beautiful love story!

Liletta Harlem

VALIDATION

THE BEAUTY OF BEING VALIDATED
Today I was heard
And it may not change the outcome
But I was heard
There were no frowns, no blank stares
And I was unapologetic with my cares
And my problem isn't fair
But I was heard
And that doesn't make me hurt less
Or feel less stress
And there still may be a no
To my yes
But I was heard
And sometimes
That's the win....

I WANT TO

FRIENDSHIP LOVE
I want to get with
sitting with you.
As I'm sitting with
getting with you.
And now I get what
you've been through.
But I don't get that-
because your you
And I bet that
because your you,
that your pain is
multiplied by two.
Which hurts me
because it's you.
But just know that
I'm here with you.
Through the storms
I got you boo!
And when need be
I'll pray with you.

Liletta Harlem

        And if you need me
        I'll stay with you.
        Because we're friends and
        that's what friends do!
        And
        Because your you
        And
        I love you!

Liletta Harlem

YOU

BEAUTIFUL SOULS

I thought about your smile

And remembered that God created light.

I thought about your eyes

And remembered that God created oceans.

I thought about your mind

And remembered that God created the universe

I thought about you

And remembered that God is Love.

FOREVER LOVE

LOVE LETTER TO MY SPOUSE
Every conversation we have
Reminds me of why greeting cards were created
Why poets put pen to paper
Why leaves were given color
Why babies chuckle
Why waves dance along the sand
Why the sun paints the sky
Why birds sing
Why the strings of an instrument echo out a melodious ring
You see, with you- I'm reminded
That God wanted us to experience beauty
Your spirit confirms that the Almighty is an artist
And with you, he has created a masterpiece
Because of you
I'm reminded why He has given us eternity
Because serving him with you
Should be timeless

AUTUMN

"Autumn, a time for preparation and the beauty of change!"

CLOSURE

So, they told me that I should write out my feelings
and that maybe somehow, I'd feel better

the "they" was a poet, and it was a letter

well, no, maybe it was a therapist, well who cares I guess

the point is- this is my attempt at closure- at saying goodbye

no that's a lie

this is my attempt at opening a door that
will close all other doors

creating a space to address a past that wraps itself up
with a pretty bow and becomes my present

I should warn you- it won't be pleasant

As I write these words, I must ask myself

will this make me feel better?

well, hmm
removing dope from an addict doesn't make
them any less of a fiend
and airing dirty laundry doesn't make it clean
so, I guess we shall see...

Liletta Harlem

BROKEN VASE
THE CYCLE OF LIFE

THE CYCLE OF LIFE AND REALIZATION
I'd be the broken vase they would look up to
They'd be too small to see through -
the pieces held partially by glue.
They wouldn't see the cracks that had
layer upon layer of tape-
covering over generations of mistakes
For God's sake
Please Let them not see the tape!
Their little eyes
watching with admiration
and determination
they want to shine just like me
glimmer like what they see
Because they don't see the cracks-
Until they do

As their eyes become older
And their reach becomes closer
The cracks become bolder

And I see their vision change
It's like I'm somewhat strange
And as they see me drifting from the range of perfection
I want to yell to them
"I'm the same broken vase I've always been
I didn't pretend
I tried to tell you in the end
You would see the imperfection"

And now you look at me directly
With your fresh determined sight
Blemishes no longer hidden by the dim light
of a child
You no longer want to be like me
In fact you ask, "why me ,
Why didn't I get the unbroken vase?"
You look me in my face
And I see your tears
But worse I see your fears
You didn't know how broken and fragile I was

Your taller now
You hold me with gentle hands
and you understand
You see that this broken vase was held together with Grace
You see withered tape that refused to undo

Liletta Harlem

And there's the glue
Keeping the pieces just barely in place
You smile with tears of appreciation you see a reflection and you see your face.
By God's Grace
You look down and see little eyes
watching with admiration
and determination
they want to shine just like you
glimmer like what they see
Because they don't see the cracks-
Until they do

Liletta Harlem

MY LOVE
THE PERFECT LOVE STORY!

SELF LOVE
You love me
Unconditionally
You look me in the eyes
Past the cries
Past the lies
And you love me

With you

I am safe
Never abused
Never confused
Because you love me

You accept the flaws
But you pause
To push me

Yes, you lovingly
Yet firmly
And ever so carefully
Convince me
To keep striving
To be
The best me

Like a painting on the wall
You respect my beauty
Thanking the creator
For sculpting me.

There is not
A pain you did not feel
A wound that did not heal
A promise left unfulfilled
That you did not experience with me.

When I gave up
You fought for me.
When I sold my soul for unrequited love
You bought it back for me.

You give me the love
That all good love stories end with as "happily"

You adore me
You honor me
You protect me
You love me

You are me....

FRIENDSHIP

LEARNING TO LIKE MYSELF
I like me
Don't get me wrong
I like you too
But not more than I like me
You see
I know all the battles I've won
And some
Most
No one else really knows
But I do
And I really like that
I also like how I laugh
The way my eyes close and my cheeks turn into round balls
And that's not all
It's the way I find humor in things so simple and small
Yeah, I like that
And I like that I've turned pain into purpose
Trauma into victory
Yeah me
The oldest of two

Liletta Harlem

I grew up poor

But wait there's more

Abandonment and daddy issues

Depression and attempts of suicide

It's been one heck of a ride

But that's why I like me

And only I can really make me happy

And if I must choose between me and you

I choose me

Because I'm pretty dope

And I like me

YOUR SEASON IS NOW!

EMBRACE CHANGE
When is your season?
What is the reason you decide that today is the day?
The day you embrace a snowflake on your lips,
or let your fingertips feel the rain
as you dance about
and take in the spring?
Will today be the day you sing?
Will you dip your toes in the sand?
And allow the waves to carry you as far as they can?
Look up at the colors on the trees
Feel the fall breeze across your face
Make today the day you embrace it all,
Today, right now. this is your season
Today is the day you say I AM

Made in the USA
Middletown, DE
17 February 2023